Call Him Father

How to Experience the Fatherhood of God

Rev. Edward G. Maristany

Scepter Publishers

Scepter Publishers, Inc.
info@scepterpublishers.org
www.scepterpublishers.org
800-322-8773
New York

Printed in the United States of America
   First printing 1999
   Second printing 2001
   Third printing 2003
   Fourth printing 2006

ISBN 1–889334–33–2

"Everyone, then, who hears these words of mine and does them will be like a wise man who built his house upon rock; and the rain fell, and the floods came, and the winds blew and beat upon that house, but it did not fall, because it had been founded on rock. And everyone who hears these words of mine and does not do them will be like a foolish man who built his house upon sand; and the rain fell, and the floods came, and the winds blew and beat against that house, and it fell; and great was the fall of it"

(Mt 7:24–27). That is Jesus' conclusion to his Sermon on the Mount, which is a wonderful presentation of the Fatherhood of God.

Making progress in your life is like building a house. The more you build, the more danger you have of total collapse, unless you've got a strong foundation. Is yours strong?

Because—do not fool yourself—sooner or later the rain will fall. Yes, and the floods will come, and the winds will blow and beat against your house. Will it stand? The ground for your foundation must be humility. But you will not have to dig too deep if you find rock. And the rock is this: the sense of divine filiation. It's the joyful realization of being a child of God.

I have seen many people who built and built, but one day everything collapsed. I do not want you to be one of them. I want you to be happy. So let us work at the foundation. I'll tell you why this is important, but best of all, I'll tell you how to do it. Please take your time, think through the advice I am about to give you, and then act on it. I promise you success.

Happiness in heaven is reserved for those who know how to be happy on earth. And happiness on earth is the privilege of those who know—not just in their minds, but in their hearts—that they are children of God.

We are children of God

Every person's life is a succession of highs and lows, of achievements and failures, of joys and sorrows. Some people will tell you that the sum total of these things defines who you are as a person. Do not believe them. Those peaks and valleys do have an impact on you, but they do not define who you are. The only thing that defines the grandeur of your personhood is this: you are a son or daughter of God.

What can anyone achieve that is comparable to that? Physically every one of us is just an intricate combination of chemicals forming a body. A body that needs to sleep one-third of the time, and that will decay and be forgotten one day. "Remember, man, you are dust and to dust you will return," we hear in the Ash Wednesday liturgy of the Catholic Church.

Saint Teresa of Avila defined the truly humble person as someone who "walks in the truth." And what is the deepest truth about yourself? God took clay from the earth and made you in his image and likeness. He gave you your being and claimed you as his own, as part of his family. He gave you a beginning and made you eternal.

This is your greatness. This is your highest dignity. Compared to this, what else really matters? Power, money, fame, or anything else you could get in this world—what is it in comparison to belonging to God's family?

Humility, then, has two components: a profound realization that you are, of yourself, nothing; and an equally profound realization that God is your totally loving and totally powerful Father.

This is the deepest truth about you. This is the magnificent scenario where your life unfolds. You are truly human only when you walk in this truth. As Pope John Paul II once said to a group of academicians (in Perugia, Italy, on October 26, 1986), you have personal greatness and dignity because of the indestructible divine image that not only is in you, but is you.

God's original plan

When Galileo said that the earth revolves around the sun, some Church authorities got nervous and told him to keep quiet. Why? Their concern was not about a scientific truth or belief. It was about a much more important truth that they (erroneously) feared was being challenged: namely, that the human being is the center of the visible creation. The Church, you see, cannot assent to any relegation of human beings to the sidelines, or to ultimate irrelevance. The *Catechism of the Catholic Church* puts it bluntly: "God created everything for man."[1] We human beings are the center of the universe because we, and only we, are made in the image and likeness of God. No other creature bears in its nature the divine imprint. "Man . . . is 'the only creature on earth that God has willed for its own sake,' and he alone is called to share, by knowledge and love, in God's own life. It was for this end that he was created, and this is the fundamental reason for his dignity. . . ."[2]

The first human beings, however, were not content with the divine intimacy they enjoyed. Our first parents sought to "be like God" (Gen 3:5). In their pride they sought independence and self-sufficiency, as opposed to divine filiation. And thus a prodigal human race ran away from home and lost touch with its Father.

How could this disaster ever be reversed? From the universal disorder born of original sin, we can only be regenerated—that is, made capable of participating in the intimacy of the Trinity—by being grafted onto Christ. As Saint Josemaría Escrivá put it, Jesus Christ "has raised us to his level, the level of children of God, by coming down to our level, the level of the children of men."[3] What sin destroyed, the blood of the Son remade.

Baptism

At the beginning of his public life, Jesus came to the river Jordan to be baptized by John. "And behold, the heavens were opened to him and he saw the Spirit of God descending like a dove, and alighting on him; and lo, a voice from heaven, saying, 'This is my beloved Son, with whom I am well pleased'" (Mt 3:16–17).

Believe me, the same kind of thing happened on the day of your baptism. As water ran over your forehead, your heavenly Father gave you a look full of love and declared, "This is my beloved child, with whom I am well pleased." And he said it for all to hear. He said to your parents and godparents, to your relatives and friends, to fellow members of your parish, to the city, to the country, and to the entire world, "Let everyone know that this child is my child, and that I love very much and am very happy with this child of mine!" Your baptism, then, was actually a bigger event than your birth!

Saint John the Apostle says, "See what love the Father has given us, that we should be called children of God; and so we are" (1 Jn 3:1). And so we are! We are sons and daughters of God! By nature? No. God has by nature only one son: God the Son, engendered by the Father from all eternity and incarnated as Jesus Christ. The rest of us are sons and daughters of his by adoption.

We must realize, though, that our adoption by God is something even more complete and "real" than human adoption. When you adopt, say, a baby girl, you can give her all the rights and benefits of a natural daughter: your name, your home, your inheritance, and so forth. You can give her constant attention, sleepless nights . . . You can exert quite an influence on her character, her habits, her outlook on life. But still she is not your daughter in one sense: she does not have your blood.

The most common understanding of divine filiation among our Protestant friends is that it's like the legal adoption just described. But such an understanding falls short of the truth expressed by Saint John: the truth that "so we are." We are not just called children of God; we actually are such.

Our infinitely loving and powerful Father causes a marvelous change in us at baptism:

he truly gives us a new life. The blood that his natural Son shed on the cross is now our blood. In baptism we are given the supernatural genetic code that identifies us as divine, in the sense of being real sons and daughters of God by virtue of the blood of the Son.[4]

The Good News

If you were asked what was the purpose of the Incarnation, you might give the answer you memorized as a child: "God became a man to redeem us from sin and death and teach us the way to heaven." And this is quite correct. But it doesn't give the full picture. See what the *Catechism of the Catholic Church* says:

- "The Word became flesh so that thus we might know God's love."[5]

- "For God so loved the world that he gave his only Son."[6]

• "The Word became flesh to make us partakers of the divine nature."[7]

• "For the Son of God became man so that we might become God."[8]

Jesus came to do something and to say something. His words explained what he was doing; his works confirmed what he was saying.

What did he come to do? He came to give his life for our salvation, as the definitive proof of our Father's love for us. "Greater love has no man than this, that a man lay down his life for his friends" (Jn 15:13). He came to make us, through the shedding of his blood, his brothers and sisters—sons and daughters of God.

And what did he come to say? To find this out, just open any page of the Gospels where Jesus is teaching. What is he talking about? You may be surprised to see that he is constantly talking of his Father, and of his Father's relationship with us. Examine every story, analyze every parable and allegory, study each part of the Sermon on the Mount, and you'll find the same theme running throughout. Our blessed Lord uses all kinds of ways to get across this single piece of good news: that God is our Father and we are his beloved children. "Divine filiation," as Pope John Paul II says, "constitutes the essence of the Good News."[9]

This Good News is what the shepherds learned at the crib in Bethlehem, what the disciples learned at the cross in Jerusalem, what the apostles spread throughout the world, and what today is so much forgotten. You and I need to hear it once again, really take it to heart, and then spread it around.

A unique love

One day an ambitious young fellow said to me, "Yes, I know that I am a son of God. But so are you. Important as it seems, let's face it—it's a shared condition. I just have a hard time putting so much emphasis on something that everybody can claim."

Listen: you are, in a real sense, an only child. God has no other son or daughter that he loves the same as you. That's one reason you must never look at your adoption by God as a mere legal formality.

Imagine two sets of good and loving Christian parents, both open to any children God may wish to bless them with. The one couple has only one child. The other has six, with another on the way. Will the new baby get only one-seventh of the love that is received by that only child? Can human love be sliced up like an apple pie?

Love is spiritual, and the human heart has a tremendous elasticity. In a healthy family, a new baby just enlarges the parents' capacity for love. Each child is loved in a unique way, and with each parent's whole heart.

If we, limited as we are, can love so much, imagine what can be done by God, who is love. God loves each and every one of us in a unique way. As someone once said, "God only knows how to count to one."

What the world needs now

Consider the sad state of our society today. People thought that technology was going to make us all happy. Instead, in the last thirty years our society has fallen into depths of crime, ignorance, and moral degradation that many of us would never have thought possible. Happiness is more elusive than ever. There is a general feeling of insecurity and fear. Fear of crime, fear of sickness, fear of loneliness and old age. Fear of life and of death. Fear of what the future may hold. Fear of giving oneself, of making lifelong commitments, of burning one's bridges. And, above all, fear of not being loved. Psychiatrists and other therapists are swamped with clients. Depression is rampant.

And what is the most common self-prescribed remedy for fear? Diversion: TV, music, sex, computer games, drugs. Our generation craves diversion because it is afraid of silence. "Silence is," as Saint Josemaría Escrivá said, "the doorkeeper of the interior life,"[10] and when one allows a bit of silence into one's life, one may see that this life, one's real life, is in shambles and going nowhere. "Don't you long to shout to those youths who are bustling around you: Fools! Leave those worldly things that shackle the heart and very often degrade it . . . Leave all that and come with us in search of Love!"[11]

The knowledge and experiential sense of one's divine filiation is the very root of happiness and joy. In the words, once again, of Saint Josemaría, "If we feel we are beloved sons of our heavenly Father, as indeed we are, how can we fail to be happy all the time?"[12] When you really know you are with God your Father, you will have no fear. With him you can't fail. With him you can think straight, you can keep your mental balance, you can see and keep things in right perspective, because in relation to him everything makes sense.

Now, it may not be easy to get this truth firmly rooted in your mind and heart. First of all, you must have faith. And then you must gather the courage to confront your unhappiness with uncompromising realism, and God knows that such a move takes a lot of humility. But it is possible. God is calling you. "Come," he says, "come and I will show you who you are."

Experiencing the reality

One day a six-year-old girl asked her nine-year-old sister, "How come some angels became devils?" Her sister, going straight to the heart of the matter, answered, "Because they wanted to be God." The little one shook her head and said softly, as though to herself, "But it's enough to be his children!"

I'm sure this little girl had no theoretical knowledge of "divine filiation." But she had the sense, the instinct of it. Her heart was joyous because she could feel, without a shred of fear, the reality that God was her Father.

Let me say it again: it is not enough to know that we are children of God. Millions of people know it and still live in darkness. Many who could give lectures on the subject have not made divine filiation the foundation of their spiritual lives. And as a result, their spiritual lives are shaky.

Now, this six-year-old girl came from a large and devoted family, and I'm sure it was her relationship with her parents—the warmth and tenderness and security of it—that made her able to feel the reality and joy of being a child of God. The most important spiritual mission of parents is to enable their children to feel the love of their heavenly Father. We could even say that God wanted

us human beings to come into this world
through the cooperation of parents precisely
so that our parents could instill in our hearts,
through their love for us and through the example of their lives, a sense of how much
God loves us.

The role of parents

One of my earliest memories centers on a
rented house in the mountains where we spent
our summer vacations. It was too far from
his place of employment for my father to
commute, so he stayed in the city all week
and then joined us for the weekends.

We always had lots of fun. In a family of
seven children, you're never bored. But Fri-
day evenings were the best. Our playing was
filled with a happy sense of anticipation. We
played more quietly than usual, because we
wanted to hear our dad's car coming in. We
knew he would honk as soon he came around

the last curve. And the instant he did, we dropped everything and let out a whoop of joy and raced to the gate, arriving there before the car came to a stop. To find my mother, he would have to work his way through that barrier of filial affection.

It is the role of a father to introduce each child to the love of our heavenly Father. In the decisions he makes as head of the family, in his way of answering a question, in his unselfish way of acting, in the hugs and protection he gives his children, a good father becomes the natural reflection of the wisdom and love, the power and providence, the mercy and forgiveness of God.

Another simple example, from the life of another young family. Every morning the father, before awakening his wife, sits in their living room, reads from a spiritual book, and spends a few minutes in mental prayer. He wants to be alone, but, he says, "it is not unusual for one of my three boys to wake up early and stumble into the living room while

I am praying. They know I am praying and will just snuggle in my lap quietly. Sometimes one will want to say a prayer or ask me a question about God. That's fine—another voice in the conversation."[13] Is there any doubt that each of these boys will grow up in a happy awareness of his divine sonship?

One more example, from a slightly different perspective. It was a grandfather's 99th birthday. All of his children, with their families, came together to celebrate it. One of them thanked him, in front of everyone else, for the great spirit of freedom in which he had brought them up. The old man shrugged off the compliment. "I always felt," he said, "that you were more God's children than my own. So I just stood back and watched the show!"

For acquiring naturally a sense of one's divine filiation, there is no substitute for a close father-child relationship. To acquire this mindset on one's own requires great personal effort, both psychological and spiritual. So if you have been blessed with a good and close relationship with your earthly father, that's your best place to start. Let yourself feel once again all that warmth, trust, and security, but this time in heart-bondedness with your heavenly Father, who loves you in that same way, only infinitely more so.

But if you do not have this experience to fall back on, don't worry. There are several other helps available to all of us—helps so powerful that if you take advantage of them, you will come to feel the joy of being God's beloved child.

The role of the Holy Spirit

Romans 8 will give you a boost whenever you need one. This is where Saint Paul explains the role of the Holy Spirit in our relationship of divine filiation. "All who are led by the Spirit of God," he assures us, "are sons of God. For you did not receive the spirit of slavery to fall back into fear, but you have received the spirit of sonship. When we cry, 'Abba, Father!' it is the Spirit himself bearing witness with our spirit that we are children of God. . . . Likewise the Spirit helps us in our weakness; for we do not know how to pray as we ought, but the Spirit himself intercedes for us with sighs too deep for words" (Rom 8:14–16, 26).

Saint Paul says much the same thing in Galatians as well: "God has sent the Spirit of his Son into our hearts, crying, 'Abba, Father!'" (Gal 4:6). "Abba" means "Daddy," or "Papa." It's what little kids in Jesus' day called their fathers—and what Jesus himself, in the fullness of his maturity, called God during his agony in the Garden of Gethsemane (see Mk 14:36). So here is one simple thing you can do: call God "Daddy," or "Papa," or whatever feels comfortable to you, and just relax in his presence. Don't worry about saying the right thing. Remember that the Holy Spirit is always right there behind you, knowing what is in your heart and ready to say it for you if you can't.

The role of Jesus

The apostles spent three years with Jesus, witnessing every aspect of his life—his preaching, his miracles, and all the little things. And everything he said or did unfolded the secret of his Father's love for each one.

When his passion and death drew near, and a feeling of sorrow was in the air, Jesus tried to comfort his apostles by revealing to them yet another thing about his Father. "Let not your hearts be troubled," he said. "In my Father's house are many rooms. . . ." But Philip, thinking he'd had enough of just hearing about the Father, said to Jesus, "Lord, show us the Father, and we shall be satisfied." And Jesus said to him, "Have I been with you so long, and yet you do not know me, Philip? He who has seen me has seen the Father . . ." (Jn 14:1–11).

One easy way, then, to get to know the Father is to read slowly and attentively everything written about Jesus in the Gospels. Let yourself feel the impact of every little thing he said or did. Because if you do take the time to really hear and see things I assure you that you will feel them, you will feel your heart come alive with love from and for Jesus, and you will in that way come to feel the joy of being a beloved son or daughter of your heavenly Father. I especially recommend that you read, reflect on, and thoroughly take to heart Jesus' story of the prodigal son (Lk 15:11–32). Do this as often as it takes—every day, if need be—to program into your subconscious this image of how your heavenly Father actually feels about you. You may feel it's too good to be true, but Jesus is here to say it is true, so it's time to believe it and start living in the sunshine of it.

Another simple way you can get to know the Father is to approach Jesus in the three moments in which he appears most defenseless:

• In your mind, go up to the crib in Bethlehem and take Jesus in your arms. Kiss him, rock him, sing to him. Then raise your eyes to your heavenly Father and put this child, and yourself, in his arms.

• In your mind, go up to Calvary and take the lifeless body of Jesus into your arms. Let yourself get soaked with his blood. Stroke his hair, clear his eyes, pick the thorns out of his head, one by one, and feel his still-warm flesh. Then look up and see how moved the Father is by his Son's sacrifice and your union with him.

• Receive Jesus in the Eucharist. There can be no greater self-giving than what Jesus does here. When you get back to your pew, dissolve yourself in words of love. Then look up and say to the Father, "Father, look at me now, because now I am worth looking at. Because now it is not I who live, but your Son who lives in me."

"Give thanks often to Jesus, for through him, with him, and in him you are able to call yourself a son of God."[14]

"The key to intimacy with the Father, the Son, and the Holy Spirit is to follow Christ in such a way that we not only imitate but identify ourselves with him. Only thus is Jesus the firstborn among many brethren while still the only-begotten Son of the Father. We aren't the Father's children each on our own account; while still ourselves, we are his children because we are Christ."[15]

But remember, when you call God "Father," he has the right to reply, "I have only one Son: Jesus Christ. I hear myself addressed as Father, so where is the Christ who is calling me by this name?" Your call to divine filiation is a call to be another Christ, so to speak, in your own unique way. What a privilege, and what a challenge!

The role of Mary

Bishop Fulton J. Sheen, in *The World's First Love* (1952, 228–33), gives a superb illustration of the role of Mary in our relationship with God the Father:

"Every mortal one of us remembers the day when mother said she was going to bake us some cookies. Her plan was that we should enjoy them together. We saw her prepare the eggs, the soda, the flour, milk, sugar, butter and chocolate—I hope I have left out none of the ingredients. When, finally, the batter was made and was allowed to settle, she told us not to touch it—not because she did not want us to be happy, nor because any of the ingredients of the cookies was bad, but because, in her superior wisdom, she knew that we could not be happy in anything that was not brought to full perfection.

"But some of us did taste the batter—I know I did—and that is when the trouble began. A stomach-ache resulted from the disobedience, and the cookies we were supposed to enjoy with mother were never eaten.

"This is, in miniature, what happened at the beginning of human history, and it is being repeated, with varying stress, in every soul ever since. . . .

"[But] it is not the nature of a mother to abandon those children who hurt themselves by their own folly. . . . There is something about motherhood which is synonymous with the maximum of clemency, and which prevents us from being conquered in advance through despair and remorse by giving us hope in the midst of sins. It is the nature of a human mother to be . . . pleading for her little one, asking that the child be dismissed, or saying that he is not understood, or that he should be given another chance, or that, in the future, he will improve. A mother's heart is always full of pity for the erring and the sinner and the fallen."

One day a friend of mine was praying before a beautiful representation of our Lady's dormition. Our Lady was shown lying in a glass casket, dressed as a queen, lovely to behold in her sleep, full of light and peace. This was in a small chapel, very close to the staircase leading to the crypt where the remains of Saint Josemaría Escrivá were venerated. Well, for some reason these famous words from Saint Augustine came to my friend's mind: "All the tongues of men will not honor her as she deserves, not even if all their members become tongues." And a feeling of despondency came over him. "Mother," he said to her, "I can't honor you as I wish, as you deserve." Then suddenly a distraction broke in: a little boy jumped down the stairway and landed right in front of the sleeping Lady. His eyes got very wide, and for a moment he was too stunned to move. But then he grinned, blew her a kiss, and cheerfully trotted on towards the crypt.

My friend, struck by the simplicity of what he had seen, then said to our Lady, "Yes, Mother, there is no way I can honor you as you deserve. But you are content with the simple love of a child. So, Mother, I'll love you as a child loves you. Mother, teach me how to please our heavenly Father."

The Blessed Virgin Mary is the best daughter of God. She is also there by the crib, by the cross, by the tabernacle. She helps us learn who we are in relation to our Father God: children bursting with pride in him, and with love for him. "My soul magnifies the Lord, and my spirit rejoices in God my Savior, for . . . he who is mighty has done great things for me, and holy is his name" (Lk 1:46–49).

Here is one good and simple way to learn from your Blessed Mother how to live with a sense of being God's child. Get yourself a representation of the Blessed Virgin that you find attractive—a close-up of the face of Our Lady of Guadalupe does it for me. Look at it at length. See in her what it is to be utterly simple, trusting, peaceful, secure, joyful, loving, sinless. Talk to her, as a child talks to his or her mother. Ask her to make you experience the reality of being God's beloved child. Spend a few minutes every day looking at her face, conversing with her and opening your heart to her maternal love.

"Draw strength from your divine filiation. God is a Father—your Father!—full of warmth and infinite love. Call him Father frequently and tell him, when you are alone, that you love him, that you love him very much, and that you feel proud and strong because you are his."[16]

Developing the habit of piety

In one of Bill Watterson's most celebrated Calvin & Hobbes cartoons, the teacher asks at the end of a lesson if there are any further questions. She beams when Calvin, a child not known for his interest in education, raises his hand. "What is the point of human existence?" he asks. And after the teacher, understandably, refuses to answer a question so far off the subject, Calvin says, "Frankly, I'd like to have the issue resolved before I spend any more energy on this."

When we were children, didn't we want to know the ultimate meaning of things? And didn't we most want to know the ultimate meaning of love? Surely every one of us can relate to this story from Peter Kreeft: "When he was about six, my son asked me, 'Daddy, why do you love me?' I began to give the wrong answers, the answers I thought he was looking for: 'You're a great kid. You're good and smart and strong.' Then, seeing his disappointment, I decided to be honest: 'Aw, I just love you because you're mine.' I got a smile of relief and a hug: 'Thanks, Daddy.'"[17]

As that 99-year-old grandfather clearly understood, a human being cannot with literal truthfulness say to another human being, "You are mine." People cannot own other people, because we are all naturally and inalienably free. But God does own me, and he does own you, because he has made us.

The fact that he made us free does not cancel or even limit his ownership.

However, God does not own you in the same way that a watchmaker owns a watch that he has made and then put in a drawer and forgotten all about. He owns you with the possessiveness of a good father. He has made you his child and thus expects from you a love and an obedience that can only be given freely. God runs the risk of our freedom with an expectation of receiving in return the love of our hearts, the docility of our wills.

How can you show your heavenly Father that you love him? Well, why not begin by simply telling him so? Just say, "My God, I love you!" Are you worried that it won't ring true? That it will be just words, without anything real behind them? Don't let that worry you. The words imply that you want to love him, and that's enough to make him happy. Actually, if truth be told, we all do more things for that reason—that we want to love—than out of a love so pure and instinctive that we just can't help ourselves. And it doesn't matter. In fact, this way may even be more pleasing to God.

Now let's ask the question again: How can you show your heavenly Father that you love him? Just do the regular things any son or daughter does in relation to a wonderful father:

• talk to him trustingly, completely opening your heart to him;

• call upon him in a time of need;

• tell him something that's hard to say;

• ask him to explain something you don't understand;

• tell him about your day, about the important things and the trivial things;

• tell him about your friends;

• obey him;

• keep him company;

• by your little victories in life, make him proud to be your father;

• when you've done something wrong, approach him with sorrow—not for fear of the punishment you might get, but for having displeased him;

• quietly snuggle in his lap, telling him with just your presence and your eyes, "I belong to you, and for this reason I am the happiest person in this whole world."

In such simple ways as these, we develop into a habit our gift of piety, which is one of the seven gifts of the Holy Spirit. Now let's take a more detailed look at a few activities and attitudes that can help keep our hearts properly attuned, deepen and enrich our relationship with God, and protect us from any temptation to pride.

Prayer

Who do you talk to when you pray? When you spend some time in meditation, who do you address? The Father? The Son? The Holy Spirit? Or just the generic "God"? Or is it all three Persons, plus maybe Mary, your guardian angel, and a few favorite saints? Let me put it this way: Who catches your attention most often?

We know who caught Jesus' attention. When he was asked, point-blank, how to pray, he did not hesitate: he told us to address the Father. "When you pray, say: 'Father, hallowed be thy name . . .'" (Lk 11:2). He also said, "When you pray, go into your room and shut the door and pray to your Father who is in secret; and your Father who sees in secret will reward you" (Mt 6:6).

Do you want to develop a sense of your divine filiation? Then, in your times of prayer, address first the First Person of the Blessed Trinity, God your Father.

Meditate on this beautiful passage from the *Catechism of the Catholic Church*: "The Son of God who became Son of the Virgin learned to pray in his human heart. He learns to pray from his mother, who kept all the great things the Almighty had done and treasured them in her heart. He learns to pray in the words and rhythms of the prayer of his people, in the synagogue at Nazareth and the Temple at Jerusalem. But his prayer springs from an otherwise secret source, as he intimates at the age of twelve: 'I must be in my Father's house.' Here the newness of prayer in the fullness of time begins to be revealed: his filial prayer, which the Father awaits from his children, is finally going to be lived out by the only Son in his humanity, with and for men."[18]

Trusting God in times of difficulty

It has been said that God the Father speaks to us through his providence, God the Son through other people, and God the Holy Spirit through no person or thing. But this is perhaps better understood in reverse order: (a) the Holy Spirit acts directly in your soul any time he wants; (b) when you obey those who rightly guide your soul, you are obeying Christ, the Son of God, whom they represent; and (c) God the Father, in turn, uses all the circumstances and events of your life to tell you his will and to draw you into the embrace of his love.

Saint Paul says "For those who love God, everything works for the good" (Rom 8:28). Everything that happens to you, whether it's within or beyond your control, comes from the loving hand of God, or is at least permitted by him. That includes nice weather and nasty weather, the healthy feeling and the pain in the back, the smooth skin and the wrinkles, the winning ticket and the layoff, the new friend and the friend who goes away, praise and criticism, joy and sorrow. Life is a play, and divine providence is the stage and the props. It is up to you to play your role to the very best of your ability.

Now, even when we do realize that absolutely everything in our lives somehow fits into God's plans for us, and that those plans are ultimately for our well-being and happiness, that doesn't make the hard and painful things easy to take. Trust in our heavenly Father often takes a lot of courage. But it is well worth the effort. As Saint Josemaría says, "We are stones—blocks of stone—that can move, can feel, that have completely free wills. God himself is the stonecutter who chips off the edges, shaping and modifying us as he desires, with blows of the hammer and chisel. Let us not try to draw aside, let us not try to evade his will, for in any case we won't be able to avoid the blows. We will suffer all the more, and uselessly. Instead of polished stone suitable for building, we will be a shapeless heap of gravel that people will trample on contemptuously."[19]

"Steps: to be resigned to the will of God; to conform to the will of God; to want the will of God; to love the will of God."[20]

God's plans cannot be improved upon. Happiness comes when we humbly and cheerfully accept the scenario God has given us, or allowed us to have, to work with.

Don't think, "What do I feel like doing?" (This is on an animal level.)

Nor, "What can I do that will be best for me?" (Selfish.)

Not even, "What does God want me to do?" (Distant.)

Say, "My Father, I know you have arranged all this for my good. What do you want me to do?" (Personal and intimate.)

If you put and keep your trust in divine providence, you will experience that unfailing joy which is the heritage of the children of God. "Cheerfulness is a necessary consequence of our divine filiation, of knowing that our Father God loves us with the love predilection, that he holds us up and helps us and forgives us. Remember this and never forget it: even if it should seem at times that everything around you is collapsing, in fact nothing is collapsing at all, because God doesn't lose battles."[21]

"Look at the birds in the air: they neither sow nor reap nor gather into barns, and yet your heavenly Father feeds them. Are you not of more value than they?" (Mt 6:26).

In the Mass

At both ends of the Mass we make a sign of the cross and invoke the Father, the Son, and the Holy Spirit. The activity of all three Persons of the Blessed Trinity is truly central to the entire liturgy. But it reaches its culmination in the Sacrifice itself, which is the essence of the Mass; for it is offered by Jesus to the Father through the Holy Spirit.

After the exultation of the "Holy, holy, holy," silence falls around the altar and a very intimate conversation begins. The priest, acting in the person of Christ, addresses our eternal Father. His words are solemn and poignant. The whole congregation speaks through him, offering to the Father his beloved Son, Jesus Christ.

You will hear the priest using the ceremonial phraseology of the liturgy: "Father, all-powerful and ever-living God. . . ." But if you want to, you can simply say in your heart, "Father!" The priest continues: "who in your infinite goodness has deigned to send your only son to be our Savior . . ." But we say it more simply: ". . .you sent Jesus to save me." And the priest concludes: ". . . .look with mercy upon your people and forgive our iniquities." Which, in turn, we simply render into: ". . .I am sorry." Doing translations like this, into language that goes straight to the bottom of your heart, can help you relate to God as the beloved son or daughter of his that you truly are.

There is no greater opportunity to experience intimacy with your Father in heaven than in the Mass. The priest should not be the only one addressing him from the altar. Yes, he is the one who stands there and says the prayers out loud, and only he is tied to the words themselves and must utter them faithfully. But you can pick up a missal or a missalette and, in your heart, say these prayers along with him, either in the same words or in your own. As a baptized Christian you have had conferred on you the common priesthood of all the faithful.[22] The Mass is the great sacramental moment to exercise this priesthood.

When the Eucharistic Prayer comes to a close, with the glorious "Through him, with him, in him" doxology, be sure to reply clearly and distinctly, "Amen!" By this "Amen!" you are saying, "Yes, in everything the priest has said, he has been speaking to me, because to the sacrifice of Christ I have united my own." And that is how you will "have the courage" to stand up and say, "Our Father, who art in heaven. . . ."

Awareness of the Father's presence

Where can we find the Third Person of the Blessed Trinity? Within us: in our soul, as long as we're in the state of grace.[23]

How about the Second Person? "In his word, in his Church's prayer, 'where two or three are gathered in my name,' in the poor, the sick, and the imprisoned, in the sacraments of which he is the author, in the sacrifice of the Mass, and in the person of the minister. But 'he is present . . . most especially in the Eucharistic species.'"[24]

And the Father? Surrounding us wherever we happen to be. "In him we live and move and have our being" (Acts 17:28). Our entire life unfolds in the company of our Father, before his eyes and under his guidance.

Should we always be attentive to our Father's presence? A constant explicit awareness of it is not possible in this life. But the sense of divine filiation can accompany us always. It's like always knowing in the back of your mind that you're not alone in the room. How differently we act when we know we are being watched—and watched by one whom we love!

Everything we do happens in this way: under the loving eyes of our heavenly Father. This reality is the very air we Christians breathe. It is the spirit that should inspire our every thought, word, action, and desire.

"It is necessary to be convinced that God is always near us. Too often we live as though our Lord were somewhere far off—where the stars shine. We fail to realize that he is also by our side—always. For he is a loving Father. He loves each one of us more than all the mothers in the world can love their children, helping us and inspiring us, blessing. . . and forgiving. . . We have to be completely convinced, realizing it to the full, that our Lord, who is close to us and in heaven, is a Father, and very much our Father."[25]

Every now and then throughout the day, exert yourself to take note—and advantage!—of the fact that your heavenly Father is keeping you company. A particularly good time to do this is at night, when you go to bed. Put the burdens of the day aside—tomorrow will be another day—to go to your heavenly Father for refuge, comfort, and love.

Becoming like a little child

In 1997, one hundred years after she died, Saint Thérèse of Lisieux was named a Doctor of the Church. And the reason was her teaching on spiritual childhood. She understood and lived it with phenomenal clarity, depth, and thoroughness, and was very good at teaching others how to do the same.

This nun loved God with every fiber of her being, but she just could not stay awake at early-morning prayer time. In her autobiography she says, "I should be desolate for having slept (for seven years) during my hours of prayer and my thanksgivings after Holy Communion; well, I am not desolate. I remember that little children are as pleasing to their parents when they are asleep as when they are wide awake; I remember, too, that when they perform operations, doctors put their patients to sleep. Finally, I remember that 'The Lord knows our weakness, that he is mindful that we are but dust and ashes.'"[26]

Such confidence and lack of anxiety can come only from a sense of one's divine filiation and a childlike way of loving. So don't be afraid to let yourself think and feel on a little-child level in relation to your heavenly Father. Remember, "Before God, who is eternal, you are a smaller child than, in your sight, a two-year-old toddler."[27]

At the same time, it is important to remind ourselves that parents count on their children to take care of some household chores and, as they grow, to take more of a role in the care of their younger sisters and brothers. Being sons and daughters of God also means being privileged with a tremendous responsibility. We belong to a universal family, and our heavenly Father has arranged things in such a way that our contributions are vital. He didn't have to need us, and, of course, in a strict sense he doesn't. However, he loves us so much that he gratifies even our need to be needed. He has chosen, in some real sense, to actually depend on us.

On May 14, 1987, Pope John Paul II said this to a group of young people in Holland: "People become really human only when they know how to meet the demands which are laid upon them by the dignity which arises from their having been created in God's image." A good meditation on that statement can give us a healthy, balanced sense of our divine filiation. It can give us an attitude that is childlike without being childish.

Contrition

Jesus used every opportunity to convey to us the incomparable love and lovableness of our heavenly Father. He spoke about him all the time, extolling his providence, his wisdom, his power, his justice, his compassion. But his best portrait of the Father highlights his amazingly generous willingness to forgive.

At this point I can't do better than encourage you to read again the parable of the prodigal son (Lk 15:11–32). But this time, focus more on the prodigal son—on his change of attitude. You will see that it took a while for this young man to come to grips with the truth that the horrible situation he was in was his own fault. In fact, he didn't do this until he had literally no other choice. But when he did hit bottom, he saw that all his problems had the very same cause: he had sinned against the most loving father in the world; he had gone against him in every way.

And what did he do then? He did not despair. He did not say, "There is no way he could ever forgive me or love me again." He knew what kind of father he had. Or at least he knew to some extent. He had no idea he would get hugged and kissed and be given a big party, but he did know his father was a good man, and he put real confidence in that goodness.

We do know what that young man, at that point in the story, did not know. We know that no matter how low we have sunk, our Father is awaiting our return with open arms, ready to run out to meet us the very instant we make a move in his direction. Yes, we must have that honesty and humility that this young man had. We must shuck off all our excuses and say to him, "Father, I have sinned against you, and I know I don't deserve to be called your child." But we do need to think in those terms—in those relational, father-and-child terms. We need to be really sorry and really confident for the very same reason: because we know that the Father we have treated so shabbily loves us so much.

Working with a right intention

Don't forget, though, that the prodigal son had a brother—and he also needed repentance. After reading the whole story, ask yourself: Which of the two brothers reflects my personal situation before God? The one who runs away or the one who stays at home? I would guess that you will find yourself reflected in both.

Through the younger son we learn that being with God is the only way to be happy. Through the older son we are reminded that we will still be unhappy if we stick with God for the wrong reasons. We must work for him, but not like mercenaries who sell their services to the highest bidder. We must work as sons and daughters, laboring cheerfully in a family concern. "All that is mine is yours,"

God tells us. In this life, there are many good reasons to work: to sustain oneself in dignity, to attend to the needs of one's relatives and friends, to fulfill one's role as spouse or parent, to help meet the needs of the Church and of the less fortunate. But the ultimate reason, and the one which gives meaning to all the rest, is to please God our Father by helping to make it happen that his Son Jesus Christ, through the power of the Holy Spirit, will reign in all human activities.

Such an end calls for a lot of rectifying. During your work, lift your heart to God often, telling him something like this: "God my Father, I offer to you this work. I do this because I know—and I'm so happy to know!—that you are Lord of all creation. And I do it as a way of making up to you for my sins against you, and for other people's sins against you. And I do it as a way of becoming holier, more a true child of yours. Help me, my Father, to do a job really worthy of you."

Two dangers

Having discussed some of the activities and attitudes that foster the sensing of our divine filiation, we now need to look at a couple of things that pose a serious threat to it.

The devil, knowing far better than we do the value of the virtue of piety, is definitely going to try to snatch it away from us. But he is smart enough not to show his cards, just as he does not show his ugly face. He knows that any direct attempt to buy us off from loving God would backfire. He knows that his presence is so revolting that any sensing of it would scare us straight into the arms of God.

So instead, he will try to use the complicity of your own fallen nature. He will try to derail you into activism and routine, and goad you from there into self-pity and despair.

Let's take a closer look at those two allies of the devil, activism and routine.

Activism. For a period of time, the demands of your job may seem to be the most important challenge of your life. The appeal can be awfully strong. Adrenaline keeps you going. You can easily get addicted to urgency—to that all-absorbing and ever-increasing need to get a lot of things done, to show results, to catchup with the backlog, to prove you can do it. It's exhilarating, it makes the time fly by. But soon you get to the point where you have no room in your day for a heart-to-heart talk with God, no time when you can chuck everything else and just be with him.

If you don't fight this pull toward activism, then your prayer—what is left of it—will become an obsessive monologue, and the memory of being a child of God will fade in the wake of your self-centeredness.

How can you prevent this from happening?

a) Remind yourself often that God must come first, and that the best time of the day should ordinarily be reserved for him. You have your priorities way out of order if you put off prayer till the very end of your day, when you're worn out.

b) During your work, make yourself pause from time to time to recall that you are in the presence of your Father God, and to try to see things from that perspective. Stop at noon to pray the Angelus. Take a minute or two after hanging up the phone, or after signing a letter, to lift up your heart to the Lord. If you can't get a moment's peace and quiet any other way, take advantage of your time in the restroom! Do something to break the momentum. When your eyes hurt or your back aches after hours of work, tell your Father that you love him, and that this is all for him. Take a deep breath, deep enough to absorb God's presence, deep enough to recover the big picture. And when the time comes to stop your work, stop it. God wants his child with him somewhere else.

Routine. "Flee from the routine as from the devil himself. The great means to avoid falling into that abyss, the grave of true piety, is the constant presence of God."[28]

Piety, to prevail, needs to be nurtured every day. The fire of love needs to be fed constantly; new fuel has to be thrown in. Whether a big log or just a twig, something has to be sacrificed to keep your soul alive for another day, to keep it brightened and warmed by the love of God.

At times your feelings of love for God and of closeness to him will disappear. Your struggle will become more difficult. Your heart won't seem to be responding. Supernatural things will give you little pleasure, and your dedication will be harder to maintain. When that happens, remember that spiritual dryness is not an enemy, but a trial. If you quit praying because no feeling comes along, your rectitude of intention leaves much to be desired. If, on the other hand, you persevere in prayer, you prove that you are there not to receive consolation, but to console this God of ours who is so basely treated by his degenerate children (see Deut 32:5).

"You must be constant and demanding with yourself in your regular practices of piety, even when you feel tired and arid. Persevere! Those moments are like the tall red-painted poles which serve as markers along the mountain roads when there are heavy snowfalls. They are always there to show where it is safe to go."[29]

Conclusion

"Presence of God, awareness of our divine filiation; everything else is a way of achieving this."[30] It is not sufficient for you to know that you are a child of God. You need to experience that relationship, nurture it in your heart, and develop it throughout your spiritual journey. At each stage of your life the consciousness of your divine filiation, the joyful realization of being a son or daughter of God, should be the atmosphere in which your life unfolds. It should permeate every thought, word, and deed.

Put all this into practice yourself, and then teach it to others. For this is your greatest apostolic mission: to help those around you to learn how to pray, how to live from within their divine filiation. Once your friends develop this habit, the virtue of piety, they will seek supernatural grace—energy, power—on their own. You give them a jump start, and they will learn how to recharge their own batteries. You teach them where and how to lay the foundation of their spiritual life, and the grace of God will do the rest.

Set firmly this foundation. It is the best guarantee of final perseverance: God won't fail to give that grace to those who rejoice in being his children, regardless of their miseries. It is also the best way to secure the hundredfold in this life: the peace and joy of the children of God in the midst of the world. Never forget this: "The best way of showing our gratitude to God is to be passionately in love with the fact that we are his children."[31]

Endnotes

1. *Catechism of the Catholic Church* [*CCC*], no. 358.

2. *CCC*, no. 356; *Gaudium et Spes*, no. 24.

3. *Christ Is Passing By*, no. 21.

4. See Rom 6:3–4, Eph 2:11–13, and Heb 9:13–14.

5. *CCC*, no. 458.

6. *CCC*, no. 458; Jn 3:16.

7. *CCC*, no. 460; 2 Pet 1:4.

8. *CCC*, no. 460; Saint Athanasius, *De Incarnatione Verbi*, 54.3.

9. *Crossing the Threshold of Hope*, 1994, 21.

10. *The Way*, no. 281.

11. *The Way*, no. 790.

12. *The Forge*, no. 266.

13. Mike Pakaluk, "Opus Dei in Everyday Life," *The Family* magazine.

14. *The Forge*, no. 265.

15. Fernando Ocáriz, *God as Father*, 1994, 18.

16. *The Forge*, no. 331.

17. *Fundamentals of the Faith*, 1988, 185.

18. *CCC*, no. 2599; Lk 1:49, 2:19, and 2:51; Lk 2:49.

19. *The Way*, no. 756.

20. *The Way*, no. 774.

21. *The Forge*, no. 332.

22. *CCC*, no. 1268.

23. See *CCC*, nos. 703, 1265, and 1266.

24. *CCC*, no. 1373; Mt 18:20; Mt 25:31–46; *Sacrosanctum Concilium*, no. 7.

25. *The Way*, no. 267.

26. *Story of a Soul*, 1976, 165; Ps 103:14.

27. *The Way*, no. 860.

28. *The Way*, no. 551.

29. *The Forge*, no. 81.

30. Blessed Josemaría Escrivá, Instruction, May 1935–September 14, 1950, note 28.

31. *The Forge*, no. 333.